MINI-GUIDES

BATTLE OF NORMANDY.....

First Victories

June 7 - 30, 1944

Alexandre THERS

Lay-out by the author - Computer drawings by Antoine POGGIOLI
Translated by Jonathan NORTH

h&c
PARIS

CONSOLIDATION

By the evening of June 6, 1944 it was apparent that the Normandy landings had been successful. The Atlantic Wall had been breached. But the campaign was by no means over and, indeed, the Allies had not yet achieved their initial objectives. Among these was the great city of Caen. Above all, Allied forces were now vulnerable to a German armored counter-attack. The Allies now faced a massive undertaking: they had to link one landing beach to another, making sure the Germans would not be able to drive a wedge between the various beachheads. They had to consolidate their gains, create airfields, set up artificial ports or capture harbors and, by so doing, guarantee their supply route.

Among the many tasks awaiting the Allies in Normandy, one of the most important was securing the actual beachheads. Here, US mortars do just that at Utah.
(National Archives)

A sleeve patch of the US 1st Army.
(Militaria Magazine)

Inland from Utah an amphibious Sherman, belonging to the 70th Tank Battalion, encounters a wagon full of German prisoners.
(National Archives)

AMERICAN ZONE, JUNE 7 - 8

General Omar Bradley's 1st Army, composed of VII and V Corps, held the western sector of the front. Their principal objective was to cut off the Cotentin peninsula and then push northwards and capture the port city of Cherbourg. Simultaneously, they were to drive southwards, link up with the British and catch Generaloberst Friedrich Dollmann's 7th Army in a trap. But, Dollmann's chief-of-staff, General Max Pemsel, ordered his 84th Corps, commanded by General Erich Marcks, to react. It did, to the best of its ability, and began a series of localized counter-attacks.

Utah Beach

The American 4th and 90th Infantry Divisions arrived in Sainte-Mère-Eglise at around 12.00 and linked up with the 82nd Airborne.

GEORGIEN

The nationality insignia carried by Georgian troops serving in the Wehrmacht. It was worn on the right arm. (Private Collection)

....

Left: a lieutenant belonging to the 795th (Georgian) Battalion has surrendered to GIs of the 4th Infantry Division. (National Archives)

Collar tabs worn on campaign by an infantry officer in the German Army. (PS Collection)

....

Below: Special marker flags used by the Americans to show the location of mines in a minefield. (Militaria Magazine)

The Americans began to clear out the surrounding area and captured around 300 prisoners, most of them former Soviet prisoners of war serving in the 795th (Georgian) Battalion. Initially German counter-attacks in this sector met with a measure of success but, by 17.00, they had largely been beaten back, elements of the retreating forces falling back to Montebourg. The sector to the north of Sainte-Mère-Eglise was now swept clean of German troops and, by the evening, the constantly reinforced American troops held a 3-mile sector from Neuville-au-Plain to Chef-du-Pont. In an attempt to prevent attacks from the north, the Americans also secured the lock gates at Angoville-au-Plain near Vierville and the bridges over the canal between Carentan and the sea. Elements of the 4th Infantry Division then pushed northwards aiming to seize the coastal batteries at Saint-Marcouf and Azeville. They came under attack from the Germans in the evening and dug in for the night. In the southern sector Major General Clarence R. Huebner's 1st Infantry Division and Major General Walter M. Robertson's 2nd Infantry Division, sweeping in from Omaha, made progress towards Carentan. American paratroopers met fierce resistance at Houesville and also at Saint-Côme-du-Mont, the last strongpoint before Carentan proper. Only on the next day was the garrison of Saint-Côme-du-Mont flushed out by the 101st Airborne.

To the northwest of Sainte-Mère-Eglise German troops were pushed back to a position along a line running from Magneville to Ecausseville. The batteries at Saint-Marcouf and Azeville continued to resist, however, the former finally being overcome by the Allies. Ozeville and Quinéville became the next Allied objectives. But, as the Allied troops advanced towards these tar-

gets they ground to a halt before stiff resistance from the German 243rd and 709th Divisions at Fontenay-sur-Mer. The advance continued, however, towards Montebourg. Meanwhile Joganville and Carquebut fell to the Allies as counter-attacks launched from the east proved ineffective.

Omaha Beach Sector

Pushing out from Omaha Beach, men of the 29th Infantry Division under Major General Charles H. Gerhardt headed westwards to support Lieutenant Colonel James E. Rudder's Rangers at Pointe-du-Hoc and linked up with troops working their way inland from Utah. They also pushed eastwards in an attempt to make contact with the British pushing west from Gold Beach. Americans from the 1st Infantry Division, the celebrated "Big Red One", after some 10 hours of fighting, finally beat their way into Colleville-sur-Mer with the help of armored support before encountering the German 352nd

Division near Formigny and the 716th Division position to the south east of Route Nationale 13. This road was of particular significance because it was the only major thoroughfare and supply line running parallel to the coast and along the front lines. The Americans soon crossed it and pushed quickly forwards, fighting off the German 352nd Division. Engranville was reached at around 14.00 but its defenders held out until the evening. Mandeville also came under attack and was taken by midnight. Troops attacking from the west took Houteville and Mosles on Route Nationale 13. This latter place fell during the evening and patrols were sent off in the direction of Tour-en-Bessin, further east and just a few miles from Bayeux.

Meanwhile, a battalion of infantry supported by armor from the 745th Tank Battalion (1st Infantry Division) headed east along the coastal road and reached Huppain by dusk. Pockets of resistance still held out, especially around Vierville-sur-Mer where enemy snipers and artillery rendered the beach dangerous, causing the loss of quite some Allied equipment. The support column sent out to Pointe-du-Hoc also found itself the target of artillery and was unable to move forwards that night. The following morning, supported by the destroyer USS Ellison, and reinforced, the Americans advanced. Linking up with Rudder's Rangers at 12.00, they took the position. The Rangers, supported by elements of the 29th Infantry Division, then headed for Grandcamp. The warships HMS Glasgow and USS Texas had been bombarding the town and the surrounding area but fired their last salvos at 17.00. Resistance was quickly overcome as night fell. Even so a few hundred yards from the town a battery of 88mm anti-aircraft guns, which also excelled as anti-tank guns, brought the bulk of the 116th Infantry Regiment to a halt. It took two further days to push through to Gefosses just two miles to the west.

Further south, German regular army troops near Isigny withdrew during the night before the US advance. The Americans were now less than eight miles from Carentan. V Corps now prepared to launch an attack on June 9 and so the 1st Infantry Division secured the necessary jumping-off points along the line Moulagny–Courtelay–Grivilly–Cussy. Tour-en-Bessin, which lay in the main line of attack, fell by midday but German troops had only been expelled from the village itself and were

The Mauser 98k, standard rifle of the German Army. This one has been fitted with a Zielfernrohr 41 sight much favored by snipers. (Vincey Museum Collection)

In this newly liberated village, American soldiers chat with Norman farmers. At their feet lies a German corpse. (DR)

A Feldhaubitze 18, 150mm caliber howitzer. Seen here in pre-war camouflage, this was a standard piece of German divisional artillery. (DR)

7

*F*ield Marshal Bernard Law Montgomery was an austere and independent individual, jealous of his prerogatives. He commanded ground forces during Overlord. Seen by some as too prudent, his relationship with Eisenhower was tense but he was popular with ordinary soldiers.
(IWM)

still in the vicinity. There were isolated pockets of German troops behind the American lines, especially at Etreham. The area around Tour-en-Bessin and Vaucelles now witnessed the link up of the Americans from Omaha and the British from Gold. The US 1st Army and the British 2nd Army had joined forces.

Ten miles further to the west, on the road to Isigny, men from the 175th Tactical Group of the 29th Infantry Division were rolling towards the village of La Cambe. The village was taken at 05.30 and the march continued with the men on the lookout for the enemy. Suddenly, 88mm canon fire erupted around them, coming from the direction of Saint-Germain-du-Pert, and six Sherman tanks from the 747th Tank Battalion were knocked out. The village was stormed and taken, as was the radar station at Cardonville. Some more 88mm guns were also encountered at Osmanville and a break-through there by the 175th was frustrated until 19.00.

*A*bove: a Panther belonging to the Panzer Lehr Division is seen here, to the south of Bayeux, a few days after the invasion. *(Bundesarchiv)*

....

A German tanker's insignia. This pattern (2nd degree) was awarded for combat accomplished during 25 different days. *(F. Bachmann Collection)*

Isigny was not far off now and Gerhardt prepared to assault the town. Having come under naval bombardment, the town was in flames. The 115th found the Germans had cut the bridges over the Aure marshes but a patrol broke into Colombières, capturing a German garrison that had taken a real beating from the Allied naval barrage.

*G*eneral Fritz Bayerlein commanded the Panzer Lehr Division. He had distinguished himself as the Afrika Korps' chief of staff but he was also an excellent field commander in his own right. (DR)

BRITISH ZONE, JUNE 7 - 8

The primary objective of the British and Canadian divisions of General Miles Dempsey's 2nd Army was to seize Caen, the principal city in Lower Normandy, thereby making the Germans believe that the Allies would cross the Orne in a drive on Paris. By applying constant pressure on this sector, they hoped that the Germans would concentrate as many men as possible around the ancient city, thereby drawing reserves away from the Americans in the Cotentin peninsula. The Germans had the following troops available to carry out Pemsel's orders for a counter-attack: Generalmajor Edgar Feuchtinger's 21st Panzer Division, which had attempted unsuccessfully to break through to the sea but now blocked Allied access to Caen; the elite 12th SS Panzer Division (Hitlerjugend), under Oberführer Fritz Witt, concentrating on Carpiquet on the night of June 7 - 8; and, in addition, Generalleutnant Fritz Bayerlein's formidable Panzer Lehr Division was racing towards Caen from Châteaudun to join the action. Together, they would attempt to mount a counter-offensive that, it was hoped, would drive the British and Canadians back into the sea.

Gold Sector

On June 7, the British XXX Corps (49th and 50th Infantry Divisions) stepped up their push towards Vaucelles and Sully. Progress was made and the 56th Brigade, of the 50th Division, entered Bayeux and headed west to link up with the Americans coming down from Omaha. Field Marshal Bernard L. Montgomery's men also seized

*T*his soldier belonging to the 50th (Northumbrian) Division carries a Radio No 48, MK I, used to facilitate communications between the infantry and artillery. (Militaria Magazine)

The pleasant countryside of the Bocage was ideal for defensive operations. The little fields, thick hedgerows, small hills and the fact that there were 4 rivers crossing the area, the Vire, the Taute, the Douve and the Merderet, made the area excellent ambush country. This helped lightly armed infantry to conceal themselves and launch surprise attacks and it was also excellent for hiding artillery. At the same time, this countryside was completely hopeless for tanks.

Their normal ability to maneuver was totally constrained by their having to stick to the narrow roads, roads so narrow they were often unable even to totate their turrets.

Top right : a MP 40 pistol machine gun, standard issue to Wehrmacht troops. Some 228,600 were made in 1944. (Militaria Magazine)

....

Below : This Soviet Model 1938 120mm mortar, lacking its bipod, was used by the Germans. Their own Granatenwerfer 42 was modeled on this weapon. It had a rate of fire of between six and ten rounds a minute. (La Gleize Museum Collection)

....

Opposite Page : British troops in Normandy. Like its German counterpart, the British Army had problems with effectiveness. (IWM)

the opportunity along the way to take the Longues-sur-Mer battery which fell into their hands without a struggle. The link up with American forces was achieved at Port-en-Bessin. By June 8, the Germans held onto a narrow corridor between Sainte-Anne and Vaucelles, close to Route Nationale 13, which allowed them to organize a withdrawal to the south.

Juno Sector

The Canadian liberation of Courseulles-sur-Mer, as well as the fall of Port-en-Bessin, gave the Allies the two key harbors essential for the ongoing supply of the Allied expeditionary force. Further east, around Caen on June 8, Montgomery marshaled fresh XXX Corps divisions, which had just landed for an assault on the town. Relying on the 7th Armoured Division, the famous Desert Rats, and the 51st (Highland) Infantry Division, he came up with a simple plan of attack. The Scots would attack from the north and the Desert Rats from the south. He hoped that the US 101st Airborne Division would assist in the encirclement but, to his immense anger, Air Marshall Trafford Leigh Mallory refused to allow their use. Nevertheless the operation, codenamed Perch, was scheduled to commence on the morning of June 10.

On the enemy side, the Panzer Lehr Division was, on June 8, concentrated around the villages of Tilly and Juvigny to the south of Bayeux. The men of the Panzer Lehr had been unnerved and intimidated by incessant Allied air raids but the division's commander had the troops take cover among the hedgerows. This was terrain known as bocage: thick hedgerows skirting fields, sunken roads and cuttings, all of which helped camouflage troops and allowed them to melt into the terrain. This topography would have a decisive impact on the way in which the Germans and the Allies would fight the coming battle.

The same day, Feldmarschall Gert von Rundstedt had at last given Rommel command of Panzergruppe West. Rommel proceeded to concentrate his operations in a sector between the mouth of the river Dives and the area of Tilly-sur-Seulles. The German 7th

Army was left to hold back the Americans whilst General Leo Geyr von Schweppenburg was entrusted with retaking Bayeux and then, hopefully, with pushing forwards to the Channel. It was the Panzer Lehr Division which would have to bear the brunt of this mission. Because of this it would not be able to take part in the planned mass breakout towards the sea.

Meanwhile the German 716th Division, which was in a position in front of the 2 divisions of the 1st armored SS Panzer Corps tried, together with the 21st Panzer Division, to bar British and Canadian progress towards Caen. Pinned down, the 716th still clung on to some fortified positions but communications between battalions, regiments and divisions were so badly disrupted by Allied air raids that no one was sure who still held out where. The Hitlerjugend however, along with the 21st Panzer Division, now prepared to launch a counter-attack. Standartenführer Kurt Meyer, known to his men as 'Panzermeyer', reached the Ardenne Abbey with his 25th Panzergrenadier Regiment on the morning of June 7, to organize the counter-attack, and was astonished to find troops of the Canadian 9th Brigade already in the area, less than half a mile away. He resolved to attack at once, despite a complete lack of air support or the fact that armored support had not yet been brought forward. Completely unaware of the imminent danger, the Canadians continued with their mission of securing the villages of Buron, Authie, Franqueville and Carpiquet to the west of Caen. Supported by a British Brigade on their left flank, and by the guns of the cruiser HMS Belfast, the Canadians took Buron at 11.00, Authie at 12.30 and pressed on towards Franqueville and Carpiquet. Then all hell

A poster calling on members of the Hitler Youth to enlist in the Hitlerjugend Division. The division was created in Belgium in 1943 and was composed of 17 and 18 year olds. It was an elite unit and went into action for the first time on June 7, 1944. The fanaticism of these young soldiers took their Anglo-Canadian opponents by surprise; nevertheless they nicknamed them the 'Baby Division'. (DR)

....

Insignia belonging to the British 7th Armoured Division, the fabled 'Desert Rats'. (Militaria Magazine)

broke loose. The Canadian vanguard was hit by a deluge of shells and rained on by German mortars. Whilst the infantry took cover, 75mm anti-tank guns blew the Canadian's vehicles apart. Those that escaped fell back in

disorder. The 14th Field Artillery Regiment was not able intervene because it was blocked in by 9th Brigade. And, to cap it all, radio contact with HMS Belfast proved impossible.

As the North Nova Scotia Highlanders tried to reply to the German fire the 25th Panzergrenadiers suddenly hit them. The Canadians suffered heavy casualties and the village of Buron was caught up in the battle between tanks and infantry. At 14.00 contact with the navy was finally reestablished but its assistance proved insufficient. Inevitably, the Canadians had to fall back having suffered 422 casualties with 21 tanks destroyed. There was some success for the Canadians, however, when Brigadier Harry Foster's 7th Brigade, not having to contend with the German tanks managed easily to seize the villages of Secqueville and Bretteville-l'Orgueilleuse before crossing Route National 13 and also taking Plutot-en-Bessin and Norrey-en-Bessin. They even pushed as far as the railroad linking Paris to Cherbourg. On the morning of the 8th, SS-Brigadeführer Wilhelm Mohnke's 26th SS Panzergrenadiers arrived at Saint-Manvieu, half a mile from Norrey, and immediately went on the offensive. They burst through the Royal Winnipeg Rifles, dug in around Putot, destroying three companies. Only the intervention of the

A British commando. (Jean Bouchery)

....

O Opposite Page : Panzergrenadiers of the Hitlerjugend at Rots, 9 June. (DR)

24th Lancers, from the 8th Armoured Division, saved 9th Brigade from complete encirclement. Foster called urgently for reinforcements whilst attempting to reestablish the situation around Secqueville and Putot. Meanwhile, Meyer having uncovered the weakness of the Canadian left flank, decided to repeat the offensive begun at Authie the day before, thereby turning the flank of 7th Brigade. If the Germans reached Bretteville they might be able to push through the Mue Valley, relieve the Douvres radar station, and reach the coast. SS-Sturmbannführer Max Wünsche, commander of the 12th SS Panzer Regiment, commanded the units assembled for this ambitious mission. He relied upon just two companies of Panther tanks

The inferiority of Allied tanks when compared to those used by their German opponents was quickly made apparent.
Their principal weapons lacked range and found it difficult to penetrate the armor of the Tigers and Panthers. The tanks' machine guns were also less effective, the Vickers and Bren had a rate of fire approximately half of that of the German MG 34 and 42.

Opposite Page, top: the three most famous commanders of the 12-SS Panzer Division (Hitlerjugend). From left to right: Wünsche, wounded after an attack on Bretteville; Witt, killed a few days later; and 'Panzermeyer'. (Bundesarchiv)

and but few infantry. Meanwhile, the Reginas at Bretteville awaited the assault.

Kampfgruppe Wünsche set out from Franqueville as night fell. Rots, which lay midway along their route had already been evacuated by the Regina Rifles and was taken by the Germans without difficulty. The SS tanks raced on at full speed towards Bretteville. At 22.40 they suffered their first casualties as they pushed into the main street. Lacking sufficient grenadiers to provide support, and meeting heavy resistance from anti-tank and field artillery, Wünsche was forced to order a retreat. He was then wounded and it became all too apparent that the assault had failed.

In the end, the engagements of June 7 – 8 saw 12 SS Panzer Division's aim of throwing the British and Canadians back towards the sea thwarted but, like the 21st Panzer Division, they had at least succeeded in

Below : British medium 114.3mm cannon. Montgomery could count on excellent artillery; the rate of fire of the 87.6mm was so good that the Germans thought it had been adapted to fire automatically. (IWM)

halting the British and Canadian advance on Caen and had destroyed 26 Shermans for only 6 Panzer IVs lost. However, against these relative successes, Meyer's unsupported move had withheld vital resources which would have made all the difference to a general offensive.

Sword Sector

Brigadier General Lord Lovat's 1st Special Service Brigade was consolidating its position whilst 3 Commando pushed into the area to the south west of Amfreville in order to prevent further enemy infiltration. 4 Commando acted in support around Hauger whilst 45 Commando did the same to the south of Sallenelles. The only true offensive action was that of 6 Commando which destroyed some artillery around Bréville and took some prisoners. Meanwhile, 41 Commando succeeded, after brief resistance, in linking up with 46 Commando, which had taken control of the fortified bridge of Petit-Enfer. This part of the front, held by the 1st SS Brigade, would remain relatively unchanged until August 17, 1944.

The British 3rd Infantry Division, given the objective of taking Carpiquet, launched its 185th Brigade towards Lebisey but it was halted at Cambes by fierce resistance. This resistance was strengthened by the presence of tanks of the Hitlerjugend Division. The 8th Brigade, too, had problems moving forwards from Saint-Pierre, encountering impressive resistance from the Panzer Lehr Division. The 3rd Division was just as unfortunate. Having taken Cresserons, it then failed at Cambes-en-Plein, a village not far from Saint-Contest held by SS grenadiers. Their resistance blocked all hopes of a drive southwards.

On the June 8, the King's Own Scottish Borderers launched an attack between Cambes-en-Plaine and La Londe but it was foiled by men of the 25th Panzergrenadiers at Mâlon. A series of assaults on Cambes also failed. During the night of June 8 – 9, Meyer began to hit back against the British but, losing six tanks, he had to break off combat. Action along the rest of the front was limited to sending out patrols. To the east of the Orne, the Germans attempted to push

Top left: the Gold Cross awarded to those German soldiers who had the Iron Cross 1st Class and who 'showed exceptional bravery on a number of occasions'. (Militaria Magazine)

....

Above: elements of the 21st Panzer Division moving through Saint-Martin de Fresnay on their way to the coast. The Wehrmacht suffered from a chronic shortage of fuel in 1944 and the division's supporting infantry can here be seen on bicycles. (Bundesarchiv)

....

An American M4 (75) Sherman. (Model built by Chris Camilotte/ SteelMasters)

around the British 6th Airborne positions but without success. This sector of the front would remain relatively quiet until the 18 July. By the evening of the 8th, the Allies were firmly positioned in a band that stretched from the Orne to the Vire, a distance of some 40 miles.

AMERICAN ZONE, JUNE 9 - 10

Utah Beach Sector

The Americans now resumed their attacks on Azeville and their efforts were rewarded in the afternoon when the German garrison surrendered. Henceforth the centre of gravity of 82nd Airborne Division's attacks switched towards Fière. A major offensive, with the aim of establishing a bridgehead to the west of the Merderet, now began. The next day, paratroops crossed the river and pushed on towards Pont-l'Abbé. The 90th Infantry Division suffered heavy losses and dug in just west of Picauville. Meanwhile the German 1057th Regiment of Grenadiers prevented the Americans from taking Amfreville. Resistance was just as determined the next day and only around midnight could a handful of men get over the bridge on the Carentan

This GI carries a 1928 model haversack as well as a tent, raincoat and mess tin. (Militaria Magazine)

15

....

road. To the north, American troops around Saint-Floxel had to fall back in the face of a German counter-attack. Two assaults on Ozeville were also beaten back, with the loss of some tanks. It was the same story at the Fontenay chateau. At Montebourg, however, men of the 82nd Airborne managed to seize the railroad station and then managed to link up with men of the 29th Infantry Division at Auville, effectively uniting the Omaha and Utah beachheads.

At the same time, the area around Carentan had been secured, cutting off Oberst Friedrich von der Heydte and his paratroops. But, unperturbed, the German defenders awaited the arrival of Ostendorff's 17th SS grenadier division of, Götz von Berlichingen, now forming up around Thouars.

Omaha Beach Sector

Men of the 1st Infantry Division were streaming southwards along the Caen - Balleroy road. To the west, Isigny fell at 05.00, with 200 Germans surrendering. Whilst at 10.00 the Vire was crossed and contact was made with the 101st Airborne at Catz. Progress was also made to the south of Isigny and on June 9, German artillery of the 352nd Division, fighting as infantry, was brushed aside around Hérennerie. The Americans pushed on towards Lison and La Fotelaie. In the Aure marshes American engineers were busily establishing bridges so that the infantry could move forwards. The latter found Colombières seemingly deserted but a company was attacked by men of the 916th Grenadiers and had to fall back to Canchy. La Folie was reached about 23.00 and Bricqueville around the same time.

The 2nd Infantry Division (Indian Head) arrived at the front on June 9. Despite lacking heavy equipment, the division was tasked with flushing the Germans out of Trévières and Engranville. In some bitter fighting in broken terrain the Americans made very little progress. The Germans under Generalleutnant Dietrich Kraiss (352nd Division) did evacuate Trévières, leaving snipers among the ruins, and attempted to establish a new defensive line on the Elle. On June 10, American troops broke through the Cerisy forest, reaching Haute-Litée at 21.00 but encountered resistance from some German sappers. Prisoners testified that the German front was beginning to fall apart. The 352nd Division on the left was on the point of dissolving whilst the 716th virtually ceased to exist. Only pockets of the Götz von Berlichingen Division held out. Neverthe-

T he Americans found the bocage tough going. Collins, commanding VII Corps, thought that it was no less terrifying than the jungles of Guadalcanal. (National Archives)

less, despite the opportunity, the Americans hesitated and
thus lost the chance of a spectacular breakthrough. By June 11, the
2nd Infantry Division was around Cerisy whilst the 1st was in
an extended position along the Vaubadon–Agy road to the south
of Bayeux. It seemed that V Corps had achieved its objectives and
so XIX Corps now moved forwards to prepare for the next major
operation: an assault on Saint-Lô.

*General Freiherr Leo Geyr von Schweppenburg, commanding Panzergruppe West, was an excellent officer. He was preparing a counter-attack when he was gravely wounded on June 9. The operation was cancelled. He was replaced by General Heinrich Eberbach.
(DR)*

BRITISH ZONE, JUNE 9 - 10

Gold Sector

On June 9, Bayerlein launched his division against Bayeux. Despite
sustained British artillery fire, his men got to within three miles of
the town. There, intervention by Allied aircraft as well as a Canadian
attack on the Hitlerjugend, forced the Germans to halt and then fall back.
Bayerlein had been as unfortunate as Witt and, for Geyr von Schweppenburg, it was apparent that such piecemeal battles, involving the
partial deployment of forces, just would not work. Only a coordi-
nated assault, involving all three armored divisions could hope to
achieve the desired objective. Just then, however, the general was
heavily wounded when his headquarters near Thury-Harcourt was
hit in an air raid. Unable to continue his command, he passed respon-
sibility to General Josef "Sepp" Dietrich of the 1st SS Armored Corps.
An all-out attack was thus postponed and, overtaken by events, very
quickly became impossible. On June 10, Montgomery's offensive began and whilst Panzergruppe West managed to contain the
Highlanders for a few hours, they suffered heavy casualties, par-
ticularly at the hands of the RAF.

*An American paratroopers' boot.
(Militaria Magazine)*

*American sappers prepare a runway in order to accelerate the arrival of supplies and the evacuation of the wounded.
(National Archives)*

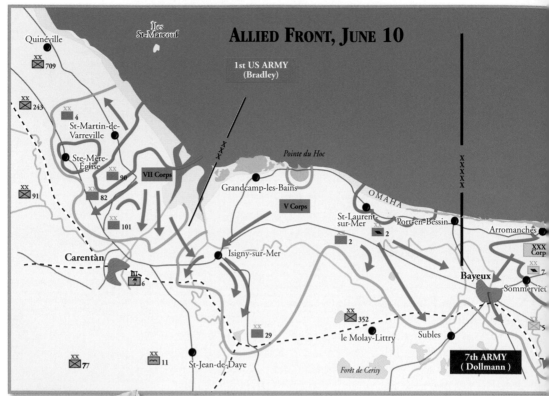

ALLIED FRONT, JUNE 10

Quinéville

Îles St-Marcouf

1st US ARMY (Bradley)

XX 709

XX 243

XX 4
St-Martin-de-Varreville

Ste-Mère-Église

XX 90

VII Corps

Pointe du Hoc

Grandcamp-les-Bains

OMAHA

XX 91

XX 82

XX 101

V Corps

St-Laurent-sur-Mer

XX 2

Port-en-Bessin

XX 2

Arromanches

Carentan

Isigny-sur-Mer

XXX Corp

Bayeux

XX 7

Sommervieu

III 6

XX 352

Subles

XX 5

XX 29

le Molay-Littry

7th ARMY (Dollmann)

XX 77

XX 11

St-Jean-de-Daye

Forêt de Cerisy

*A German poster trumpeting the defeat of the Allies. The affect of such propaganda was limited and negated by word of mouth. News of the landings spread very quickly.
(DR)*

Juno Sector

On 9 June the Hitlerjugend launched yet another assault against Bretteville. But German panzers, caught in flank by nine Sherman tanks, suffered seven tanks destroyed and the Germans had to fall back to Rots to lick their wounds. An assault on the following morning also failed. Meanwhile, north of Caen, Juno and Sword beachheads linked up. Allied progress seemed unstoppable.

Sword Sector

To the east of the Orne, Commandos beat off an attack by the German 346th Division. Following an artillery bombardment, an Allied attack was now launched against Cambes. The Allied troops suffered heavily and, despite receiving reinforcements, had to go to ground in some neighboring woods to shelter from the enemy's artillery. On June 10, the Allied lines around Caen were quiet. The Germans positions remained intact.

MORALE

In general, the Germans were certainly managing to resist the Allied advance but their counter-attacks were considerably impeded by the Allies domination of the air, something which compro-

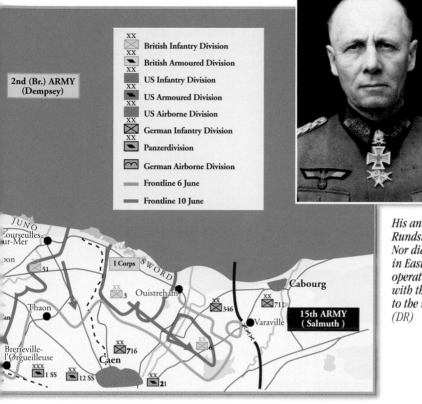

Feldmarschall Erwin Rommel commanded Army Group B. Despite the importance of the post, Rommel could not act independently. He had to work through superior officers, negotiating and persuading. His antagonism with von Rundstedt did not help either. Nor did the fact that Hitler, in East Prussia, was overseeing operations and interfering with the Wehrmacht's response to the invasion. (DR)

mised their communications and prevented movement of men and supplies during the day. Shortage of supplies and ammunition now began to take their toll. Allied control of the skies also prevented effective German reconnaissance, rendering the Germans incapable of spotting Allied concentrations and thereby gauging their plans. All attempts to break through to the sea had failed. Sepp Dietrich was of the opinion that he would need a further eight divisions just to stabilize the situation. Hitler, on the other hand, was still convinced that all he was facing was a diversion intended to pull his troops away from the Pas-de-Calais. Rommel had initially shared this point of view but now thought that a second landing was unlikely and that the 18 divisions of 15th Army should now be deployed against the Allies. Hitler refused and ordered that 'each man should fight where he stood'. He was placing all his faith in a new weapon, the V1, a flying bomb which could reach London. The first of these weapons was launched against London on June 13 and, despite British countermeasures which grew more

A German first line supply post. Fuel was a particular problem during the whole campaign as each Tiger consumed, by the different versions, between 534 and 682 liters in order to travel between 45 - 60 miles (off road). (Bundesarchiv)

A poster produced in the USA in 1944: 'the French Resistance helps throttle the Boche'.
(DR)

....

B elow : a German anti-tank mine (Tellermine 42).
(La Gleize Museum Collection)

and more sophisticated, the impact on London's morale was heavy.

For the Allis under Montgomery and Eisenhower, it was evident the German defense was being reinforced more slowly than the Allied attack. Between 7 and 12 June the Allies brought into play fifteen divisions (seven British and Canadian) against the 12 divisions Panzergruppe West and the 7th Army had on paper. The massive series of air raids had borne fruit as had the operations conducted against the occupier's communications by the French resistance. Such operations could be numbered in the hundreds and it was chiefly due to such tactics that the 2nd SS Panzer Division, Das Reich, was so delayed from reaching the front.

AMERICAN ZONE, JUNE 11 - 16

Cotentin Peninsula

American progress in the Cotentin peninsula was sufficient that Carentan fell on June 12, despite von der Heydte's defense. The German had been expecting the Götz von Berlichingen Division to arrive but it came too late to prevent the union of Bradley's VII and V Corps. General Collins, commanding VII Corps, could therefore concentrate on his main objective: taking Cherbourg. He ordered the 39th

....

General Lawton Collins commanded the US VII Corps. Nicknamed Lightning Joe, Collins was a remarkably self-assured officer. He had confidence in Bradley, the two officers having much in common, and he was one of the best commanders the Americans had in Normandy.
(National Archives)

Infantry Regiment to sweep the coast between Le Taret de Ravenville and Quinéville of isolated pockets of German resistance. Fontenay-sur-Mer fell to the Americans whilst the 4th Infantry Division swept into Ozeville and pushed through to Montebourg. This village was the lynchpin of the German defenses and was held by an assault battalion belonging to the 7th Army. By June 13, the 39th were making slow progress along a coast defended by the German 243rd and 709th Infantry Divisions. The American 4th Infantry Division continued to exert pressure but actually took precious little ground. The Germans, largely commanded by Oberst Gunther Keil since June 14, hastily pulled troops together to defend the area to the north east of Montebourg. They relied on Panzer Abteilung 100, the 919th Regiment and two companies of paratroops. Quinéville, after putting up a stout resistance, fell at 21.30 on June 15. That same day, Collins resolved to advance westwards and drive a wedge that would split the peninsula into two. His troops surged forwards, eradicating various isolated pockets of resistance. The German response was

Above left : a British Cromwell VI tank. This, along with the Sherman and the Churchill, formed the backbone of the Allied tank force. (IWM)

....

*O*pposite : a German infantry NCO wearing a field cap, model 1943, and a canvas combat uniform.
(Militaria Magazine)

Above : a V1 flying bomb. There were 61 launch sites in the Cotentin peninsula and in the Caux region on June 9.
(DR)

feeble, as all available armor had been dispatched towards Caen. So it was that the 90th and 9th Infantry Divisions, and the 82nd Airborne, took Goubersville and sped towards Saint-Sauveur. The American's westward advance continued throughout June 16.

Saint-Lô and Caumont

June 12 had also seen the beginning of V Corps' offensive towards Saint-Lô. Elements of the 29th Infantry Division had crossed the Elle between Saint-Jean-de-Savigny and Moulin-Levesque but had been chased back by superior German forces and re-crossed the river to the north. The 116th Regiment did, however, manage to take Saint-Clair around midnight; Couvains was taken the next day, at 10.45. Prisoners belonging to the 353rd Division fell into American hands. As Cherbourg was the main objective of American forces, the 29th was soon ordered to halt and hold its ground. The 1st Infantry Division attacked Caumont on the June 12 and, despite being strongly defended, it fell to them the following day at 09.00. The 2nd Infantry Division, acting along the Elle, suffered heavy casualties. On June 13 the position at Caumont was consolidated and the German 352nd Division scattered. General Marcks, commanding 84th Corps, was shot and killed when trying to rally his men and tanks to stabilize the position. General Dietrich von Choltitz succeeded him. The 2nd Infantry Division continued to operate along the Elle on the June 15, beating off a weak German counter-attack on the same day.

*Top left:
Michael Wittmann, ace of aces amongst German tankers. He began as an officer in the Leibstandarte SS Adolf Hitler but transferred to the Heavy Tank battalion of the 1st SS Panzer Corps. He was respected and feared by his adversaries.
(Bundesarchiv)*

*An advert boasting of the Tiger tank's prowess.
(Private Collection)*

*Opposite and above:
the PzKpfw VI Tiger was a monster among tanks. It weighed 57 tonnes, boasted an 88 mm cannon and had a maximum speed of 28 miles an hour (the model shows an early-type Tiger).
(Model built by Jérôme Hadacek/ SteelMasters - Bundesarchiv)*

BRITISH ZONE, JUNE 11 - 16

Gold Sector

As we have already seen, in XXX Corp's sector infantry of the 50th Division had been held in check by the enemy. Although they took Lingèvres on June 11, tanks coming to their support were less fortunate. Attempting a breakthrough between Tilly and Cristot, nine Shermans were attacked in the rear by grenadiers belonging to the 12th SS Panzer Division. Seven were destroyed in a matter of moments. Meanwhile, the Desert Rats skirted around the flank of the Panzer Lehr Division, then fighting the 50th Division, and, by 17.45, elements of the 22nd Armoured Brigade were but ten miles from Tilly. Major General Robert Erskine, commanding the 7th Armoured Division, spotted a gap in the line between the Panzer Lehr and General Heinrich von Lüttwitz's 2nd Panzer Division, just

An Oberscharführer (Chief Warrant Officer) of the Waffen SS. He wears the black uniform of the tank and armored car crews, derived from that worn by the Army (Heer). Sometimes the crews wore a black leather (naval pattern) jacket. (Militaria Magazine)

*T*his soldier carries a PIAT grenade launcher on his shoulder. Such a weapon proved devastating against Wittmann's tanks at Villers-Bocage. (IWM)

*A*llied engineers played a vital role in winning the campaign. They worked hard to restore promptly communications, especially after the devastating bombardments, and to maintain the troops' forward progress. Here Caterpillar D6s are being used by the British in Mesnil-Patry (near Bretteville-l'Orgueilleuse) to clear rubble. (IWM)

A Canadian Browning FN-Inglis No 2 Mk I pistol, 9mm caliber. It was a favored weapon among airmen and British commandos. (Militaria Magazine)

The American Colt 45 1911 A1, 11.43 mm caliber, was the standard sidearm carried by US troops. Some British units also made use of it. (Militaria Magazine)

Far left : an infantryman belonging to 3rd (Canadian) Division. This man belongs to the Regiment de la Chaumière, a unit which fought against the Hitlerjugend. Canadians generally wore British uniforms and equipment but with some modifications and a different shade of cloth. (Militaria Magazine)

then beginning to deploy. Erskine seized the opportunity and launched Robert 'Looney' Hinde's 22nd Armoured Brigade into an assault on Villers-Bocage at the summit of a small hill. Seizing this position would allow the Allies to dominate the heights and throw wide open up the Odon valley. Villers was entered on June 13 at 08.15 and Hinde then directed a column of tanks and half-tracks along the Hill 213, a road, with thick woods on either side, which lead directly to Caen. The vehicles were drawn up in a congested column when a Tiger blocked any movement further forwards by destroying the lead vehicles. Six further Tigers swarmed in for the kill and British vehicles were picked off and destroyed one by one. It was all over by 10.30. This feat had been performed by a company of SS Panzer Abteilung 1001 commanded by Obersturmführer Michael Wittmann, a hero of the Eastern Front. The German tanks then continued driving forwards, reaching Villers and, despite suffering casualties, forced the Desert Rats to retreat. Over the next two days, the British fell back towards Livry and Briquessard, five miles to the rear, covered by a massive barrage of ground artillery and air raids. In 50th Division's sector of the front no progress was made against Hottot and Cristot and only XXX Corp's prompt action in stabilizing the position on June 16 restored the situation. Some 53 Allied tanks had been lost to 40 panzers and the German lines around Caen had still not been breached.

The British operation had proved a signal failure causing as it did the whole British advance to grind to a halt. The only redeeming feature of the setback at Villers-Bocage was that a number of German tanks had been drawn into the conflict rather than being allowed to reinforce Cherbourg.

On June 16 another attempt to take Hottot failed. Nor was it possible to wrest control of the ruins of what was once Tilly, although a part of the town had been occupied. Only on the following day did it prove possible to eliminate the last pockets of enemy resistance. On June 18, Hottot was temporarily seized by the 231st Brigade (50th Division) before they were chased out again by some Panthers. Following this setback, 50th Division found itself in position along the line Livry – Lingèvres – Tilly – Saint-Pierre with the Desert Rats to the right. These positions remained unchanged until 8 July.

*S*tripes belonging
to a sergeant of the Royal
Artillery Regiment.
(Militaria Magazine)

....

*T*illy on 27 June 1944.
A British 17-pounder gun
forms part of an anti-tank
battery. (IWM)

Juno Sector

After the fiercely contested battles around Bretteville-l'Orgueilleuse, Putot and Mesnil-Patry, the 3rd (Canadian) Division licked its wounds and counted its losses. Its 8th Brigade was detached on June 11 and, in conjunction with some British commandos, was sent to comb through the Mue valley. Meanwhile, on the 12th, Rots finally fell. Having been defended by the Hitlerjugend, the place finally fell to the Regiment de La Chaudière. The following days saw the Canadians of 7th Brigade in action at Pont-à-Bessin and those of 8th Brigade around Bretteville, Norrey and Rots. The 4th Scottish-Canadian Brigade had dug in around Vieux-Cairon and came under attack from the youthful soldiers of the Hitlerjugend. The Germans, however, lost their commander, Fritz Witt, when he was hit at Venoix by a naval shell on 14 June. He was replaced by 'Panzermeyer'. The battle lines ran to the north of Caen, through Authie, Cambes-Couvrechef, Cussy, Gruchy, Buron and Saint-Contest. Action at the front was calming down, with only fighter and fighter-bomber aircraft strafing anything that moved along roads and highways.

Sword Sector

The sector of the front assigned to British I Corps was also relatively quiet. The last few pockets of German resistance, such as at Douvres and Sainte-Honorine, had capitulated. But the bulk of the British troops found themselves hemmed in between the heights

*T*his American eagle symbolizes
a victory won with the support
of War Bonds.
(DR)

which ringed Caen and the Caen canal. Although the British artillery bombarded the German positions around Caen, a spate of bad weather disrupted Allied movements. On June 19 one of the artificial harbors was destroyed in storms and that at Arromanches was temporarily put out of action. The ensuing delay played into the hands of the German defenders and they used the time to erect more and more defensive lines, to plant mines and to dig in. The situation seemed like it would turn into trench warfare. Bad weather also prevented aerial reconnaissance and the Germans took advantage of this to move fuel and ammunition up to the front in daylight.

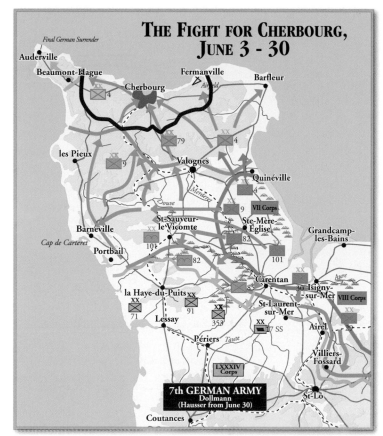

THE FIGHT FOR CHERBOURG,
JUNE 3 - 30

American Zone, June 17 - 30

The Battle for Cherbourg

On June 17, VII Corps launched its offensive westwards. The peninsula was cut in two by this operation on June 18 when men of the 9th Infantry Division reached Barneville. Collins then turned the bulk of his forces northwards, towards Cherbourg, thereby isolating what remained of the German 77th, 91st, 243rd and 709th divisions. Elements of these sought to break out of the trap but only small groups succeeded. General Heinz Hellmich, commanding the 243rd Division, and his colleague commanding the 77th, were killed by Allied air raids during this fighting. Meanwhile, Major General Charles H. Corlett's XIX Corps came into line to the left of the VII Corps and resting on the right of V Corps. On June 19, everything was in place for the launch of the decisive attack on the Norman port. Indeed taking Cherbourg was now of paramount importance to the Allied cause; supplies had diminished with the onset of bad weather and the Americans were down to two days' supplies. Major General Manton S. Eddy's 9th Infantry Division began the assault on

XX ▪	US Infantry Division
XX ⌒	US Airborne Division
XX ⊠	German Infantry Division
XX ◈	Panzerdivision
—	Frontline 3 June
—	Frontline 19 June
—	Frontline 30 June
—	German line of resistance

The Resistance played an important part in the fall of Cherbourg. They even supplied the Americans with a map of the German defenses, pinpointing precise positions. This maps was even more detailed than that used by the defending German officers.

An American grave digger. By 22 June, the Americans losses stood at 18,374 officers and men, of whom 3,012 had been killed. (DR)

The constant re-supply of the Allied forces had to be maintained given the massive demands of the invading troops. That such a flow of logistical support could be maintained was due to the establishment, on June 8, of artificial ports, built from concrete pontoon, floating platforms and breakwaters. These ports were called Mulberrys. Mulberry A, an American facility, was at Saint-Laurent-sur-Mer and Mulberry B, run by the British, was at Arromanches. The former went into operation on D-Day+3, the latter on D-Day+15. Fortunately neither the Luftwaffe nor the Kriegsmarine were in any position to attack these harbors and interrupt the flow of supplies.

the left, supported by the 79th and 4th infantry divisions in the center. The GIs found Montebourg deserted. Elements of the 24th Cavalry Group pushed on towards Saint-Vaast-La-Hougue. The Germans fell back steadily towards 'Festung' Cherbourg and were soon sheltering within the city's formidable defenses. Generalleutnant Karl-Wilhelm von Schlieben commanded the garrison of 21,000 men, the bulk of whom were within the confines of the city. On June 22, a massive bombardment heralded a general assault. American progress was excellent except for around Flottemanville – where German 88mm guns cut into the attack – and La Mare. By June 24, the Germans had been pushed back into their complex of forts. Street fighting now also began, with troops pushing through tunnels and bunkers in order to break into

Cherbourg's centre. On June 26, von Schlieben surrendered with 800 men. The entire city fell into American hands with the exception of the arsenal and the Osteck and Westeck redoubts. Finally, on July 1, all resistance ceased. Some 6,000 prisoners fell into Allied hands. In a 25-day campaign, VII Corps had destroyed or taken prisoner 50,000 Germans.

The fall of Cherbourg was the first major breakthrough in Normandy but the port was so badly damaged that it would take weeks for it to be made fully functional once again.

Bradley did not rest on his laurels. He had VII Corps move down between the VIII and XIX Corps and had his men readied for the next phase of battle: an attack between Saint-Lô and Coutances. He hoped to act quickly and thus prevent the enemy from establishing themselves in the bocage. But bad weather and difficult conditions meant that progress was much slower than intended.

Saint-Lô and Caumont

On June 15 the 2nd Infantry Division had beaten off a counterattack on Saint-Georges-d'Elle. On June 17, the Germans fell back to prepared positions and an extremely difficult phase of operations began for the Americans. Making the most of the bad weather, the Germans reinforced their troops whilst Bradley, with his supplies interrupted, had to go slow. Thanks to the work of Army engineers and the Navy's Seabees, the artificial harbors were up and running once more. By June 24 the Allies were again working at full capacity.

OPERATION EPSOM

The setbacks experienced around Tilly and Villers prompted Montgomery to devise a new operation, this time focusing on the western approaches to Caen. He now felt he had sufficient troops available for the enterprise, three army corps (XXX Corps, I Corps and VIII Corps) totaling 60,244 men, 736 guns and 600 tanks. These were under Lieutenant General Richard O'Connor. The operation, codenamed Epsom, would consist of an attack to the south of Caen, from positions four miles to the west of Carpiquet. This would not only isolate Caen but would also draw German resources away from Saint-Lô thereby relieving pressure on American forces there. But timing was essential. Montgomery knew from Allied intelligence that the Germans were preparing an attack of their own.

The first phase of the assault would consist of the 3rd (Canadian) Division seizing and holding the bridges over the Odon around Evrecy-Baron whilst 8th Corps would take up a position around Bretteville and attempt to open up the road to Falaise.

Opposing the Allies was Sepp Dietrich's 1st SS Panzer Corps, some 12,000 men with 115 heavy tanks.

These pontoons, 7 miles long, allow vehicles to pass over the marshy lands along parts of the coast. Between June 6 and June 26, 125,812 tonnes of supplies rolled ashore onto Omaha as well as 268,816 men and 40,191 vehicles. (National Archives)

On the first day of Operation Epsom, the Germans of the 12th SS Panzer Division, 21st Panzer Division and Panzer Lehr Division, in front of Caen, could field 228 tanks and 150 88mm guns and assault guns. (Bundesarchiv)

An instruction manual for panzergrenadiers, 1944. (Private Collection)

The assault was due to be launched on June 23 but was delayed by the storms in the English Channel. Dietrich took advantage of the lull by recalling Obergruppenführer Paul Hausser's 2nd SS Panzer Corps. On 25 June Operation Epsom began with a series of fixing actions on the German flanks whilst XXX Corps attacked and took Fontenay. On June 26 the attack got underway in earnest as VIII Corps surged forwards after a tremendous barrage of artillery. The 15th (Scottish) Division began by attacking towards Cheux, Le-Haut-du-Bosq, Saint-Manvieu and La Gaule. Only a few snipers belonging to the Hitlerjugend put up some resistance before being overrun. Cheux fell in the morning but Panthers of the 2nd Panzer Division maintained their grip on Haut-du-Bosq. Saint-Manvieu, reached at 08.30 was the scene of bloody hand-to-hand fighting between the Scots and the youths of the Hitlerjugend before the latter were forced to fall back. La Gaule, on the main road, also fell. Around noon the German artillery hit back as the 1st Nebelwerfer Brigade launched hundreds of rockets against Saint-Manvieu and Cheux whilst heavy mortars positioned along the Odon opened up. At 12.50, 11th Armoured Brigade burst out of Cheux and began to take casualties. It was becoming apparent that reaching the Odon was not going to be as straightforward as originally thought.

For now the Scots were stuck, hemmed in by the Germans who were masters in the art of defense. Around 18.00 an Allied brigade attempted to strike at Grainville and Colleville. In the driving rain, the Allies first stumbled against 1st SS Panzer Division before, exhausted, halting for the night. The objectives of the first phase of Operation Epsom had not been gained nevertheless morale remained high. On June 27 the RAF suspended its bombing raids as the Cloud level was too low but, to compensate for this, 3rd (Canadian) Division (acting as flank guard to VIII Corps) was able to bring into play its field artillery.

Further to the west, the British made determined attempts to break through between Cheux and Haut du Bosq but spent most of the day engaged in beating off counter-attacks by the Panthers of Das Reich. In all the Germans deployed some 140 heavy tanks against VIII Corps but did so in an ad hoc manner. By 11.00 the British had cut the road from Caen to Villers and the 'Jocks' of the 2nd Argyll and Sutherland Highlanders had reached Mondrainville near the Odon. Das Reich countered with an attack towards Cheux but it met with scant success. Throughout the day there were dozens of localized clashes but the British were building up an armored spearhead around Cheux in readiness for the

Opposite : youths belonging to the Hitlerjugend Division watch the skies for Allied aircraft. The Germans were never allowed to forget Allied air superiority. (©ECPAD/France)

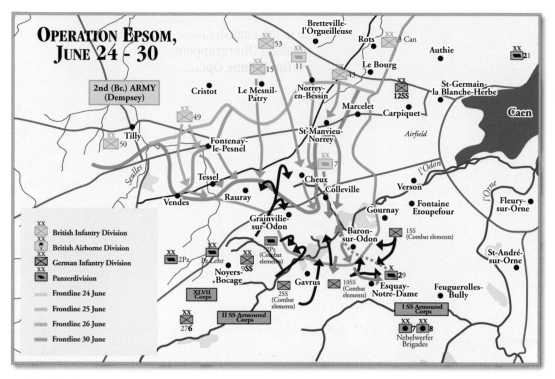

OPERATION EPSOM, JUNE 24 - 30

Bretteville-l'Orgueilleuse
Rots
3 Can
Authie
21
2nd (Br.) ARMY (Dempsey)
53
15
11
43
Le Bourg
Cristot
Le Mesnil-Patry
Norrey-en-Bessin
St-Germain-la Blanche-Herbe
12SS
49
Marcelet
Carpiquet
Caen
Tilly
50
Fontenay-le-Pesnel
St-Manvieu-Norrey
Airfield
l'Odon
Seulles
Tessel
Cheux
Verson
7
Vendes
Rauray
Colleville
Gournay
Fontaine Etoupefour
Fleury-sur-Orne
Grainvilie-sur-Odon
Baron-sur-Odon
1SS (Combat elements)
St-André-sur-Orne
2Pz (Combat elements)
2Pz
Pz Lehr
9SS
Noyers-Bocage
Gavrus
10SS (Combat elements)
Esquay-Notre-Dame
Feuguerolles-Bully
29
2SS (Combat elements)
XLVII Corps
276
II SS Armoured Corps
I SS Armoured Corps
7
8
Nebelwerfer Brigades

Legend:
- British Infantry Division
- British Airborne Division
- German Infantry Division
- Panzerdivision
- Frontline 24 June
- Frontline 25 June
- Frontline 26 June
- Frontline 30 June

push over the Odon. Finally, around 17.00 a bridge over the river at Tourville-sur-Odon fell into Allied hands. The Germans were confounded, the 2nd Panzer Division borrowing tanks from the Hitlerjugend to plug the gap. But the Allied troops were rapidly reinforced and 11th Armoured Division pushed southwest, reaching Bretteville-sur-Laize less than a dozen miles from Caen. Their next objective was to be Hill 112, the height which separated the Odon valley from that of the Orne. On 28 June, after a series of running battles, the Sherman tanks of the 23rd Hussars made it onto the heights but further progress was blocked by Tigers on the reverse slope. Artillery and aircraft joined in unsuccessful attempts to dislodge the German tanks. General O'Connor, fearing that further progress might endanger his lines of communication, ordered his tanks to stay put, making Hill 112 the most advanced point reached during Operation Epsom.

Meanwhile 15th Brigade had headed along the Odon to Gavrus, to secure the bridges there, before retreating northwards to link up with the 46th Brigade at Grainville. This effectively trapped Germans in this sector in a pocket and the ensuing battle was a merciless confrontation. Some 30 tanks belonging to 21st Panzer Division were destroyed around Mouen and Verson, most of them falling victim to Allied tanks or to the ferocious tank-busting Typhoon aircraft. On June

B elow: a Nebelwerfer rocket-launcher. It was cheap to produce, easy to use and devastating when employed against infantry. However, it wasn't very accurate and it used up a lot of ammunition. (DR)

29 the weather improved and the British prepared to meet the German counter-attack. Allied VIII Corps also prepared to meet the newly arrived 2nd SS Panzer Corps consisting of the 9th Panzer Division (Hohenstaufen) and the 10th Panzer Division (Frundsberg). But the German punch was never delivered. Decimated by artillery, naval gunnery and a raid by 250 Lancaster and Halifax bombers, the German communications were torn to shreds and the assault never got off the ground. Instead, the 129th Brigade of 43rd (Wessex) Infantry Division managed to chase the SS out of Baron whilst, on their western flank, the 44th (Lowland) Brigade seized the Grainville – Mondrainville crossroads.

But, around Gavrus, the situation was critical. The 2nd Argyll's were being subjected to deadly fire from mortars belonging to the 1st SS Panzer Division. As the 29th Armoured Brigade reached the Esquay – Evrecy crossroads, at the foot of Hill 112, it too was hit by German artillery. Then, at 18.00, the tanks of the 9th SS Panzer Division hit the 44th (Lowland) Brigade and the 31st Tank Brigade in an attempt to reach Cheux. By dusk they had succeeded but at considerable cost. The 10th SS Panzer Division, to the south of the Odon, was less fortunate, being pounded by VIII Corps' artillery at Maizet and Vieux.

Further to the east an attack by 40 Panzer IVs of the 12th SS and 21st Panzer divisions was broken up around Carpiquet by rocket-firing Typhoons. At 23.00 General Dempsey ordered his men to pull back from Hill 112, pulling the carpet from under the Hohenstaufen and Frundsberg divisions then preparing to assault the heights. Dempsey hoped to lure the Panzers into following him. By June 30, the British had consolidated their foothold on the south of the Odon and, apart from a few local successes, the German attacks had failed. The pocket formed by Allied troops between the Odon and Route Nationale 13 contained 87,000 men supported by a powerful artillery and air power. The Germans realized their chances of beating off this Allied incursion were practically non-existent.

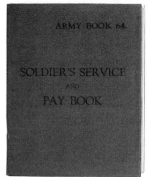

*A British soldier's pay book.
It was supposed to be carried
at all times by the soldier
and included the names and
addresses of family should
the soldier be killed. Epsom cost
VIII Corps 4,020 dead and
wounded.
(Militaria Magazine)*

Epilogue

During Operation Epsom Allied troops advanced some six miles. From the tactical point of view the operation was not a great success. Nor was the chief aim of the operation realized: the taking of Caen. Strategically, however, the move was of more consequence. The German counter-attack had been stalled and, thanks to Allied air power, the enemy had suffered irreplaceable losses in tanks. These losses meant that the Germans would now be denied the tactical initiative and put paid to hopes that the Allies would be driven back into the sea. Eight German armored divisions were now bogged down around Caen, their demoralized personnel reduced to holding their ground.

*Top left: troops belonging
to VIII Corps, composed
of the 15th and 43rd divisions,
as well as two armored brigades,
played the major role in Epsom.
The 11th Armoured Brigade was
then to rush through and
exploit the victory.
(IWM)*

The attitude of troops on either side is most revealing. For the Allies, the apparent success of the landings meant that they now felt like victors and conquerors. It seemed that the war would be over in a matter of months, even weeks, and many troops now expected the enemy would capitulate. But, for the Germans, Allied success made it more likely that any surrender would have to be unconditional. Consequently they fought back, the vision of total defeat being unacceptable.

Following Operation Torch, Eisenhower insisted on smooth relations between his subordinates and their British counterparts. Officers who didn't follow these roles found themselves sent back to the USA. (DR)

PRACTICAL INFORMATION

This list presents sites of historical interest in Calvados and neighboring regions. We are restricted to listing the most representative sites and those in the vicinity of the actual battlefields. Caen would be an excellent point of departure for any tour of the region.

CALVADOS

Five miles to the north of Caen, at Ouistreham, there is a **museum commemorating the landing of 4 Commando**. Uniforms, weapons and equipment are on display as well as documents relating to the landing of Anglo-French commandos at Sword Beach. The site is dedicated to the 177 commandos belonging to Kieffer's unit. There's also a monument alongside the D514, as it enters the south of the town, and another on the sea front.

Musée du débarquement des commandos n° 4
Place Alfred-Thomas
14150 Ouistreham
Tel.: 02 31 96 63 10

Further along the coast, 15 miles to the east, you arrive at Benerville-sur-Mer. Close by is **Mont Canisy**, transformed by the Germans into one of the most important batteries along the Atlantic Wall. There are numerous casemates, bunkers, observation posts and gun positions to visit as well as 20 miles of tunnels.

Site de la batterie du Belvédère au Mont Canisy
« Les Amis du Mont Canisy » - Mairie
14910 Benerville-sur-Mer
Tel.: 02 31 87 92 64 - Fax: 02 31 87 32 15

Opening hours: from April to October, Saturday and Sunday 14.30 to 17.30. There are free guided tours of the fortifications and installations which last 2 hours. These are given by volunteers of the Friends of Mont Canisy. There is car parking. Bring a flashlight!

Turning back towards Bayeux, the **memorial museum to General de Gaulle** recalls the great man's visits to the city. It focuses on the visit of June 14, 1944 and that of June 16, 1946. There are numerous photos and documents on display and films are also shown.

Musée-mémorial du général de Gaulle
10, rue Bourbesneur
14400 Bayeux
Tel.: 02 31 92 45 55 - Fax: 02 31 51 28 29

Opening hours: March 15 to November 15, 09.30 – 12.30 and 14.00 - 18.30.

The **largest British cemetery** of World War II is to the south of Bayeux. It contains the graves of 4,648 Allied and German soldiers, of which 3,935 are British. Heading west along Route Nationale 13, the visitor will reach the vast **La Cambe cemetery**. Here 21,500 German soldiers lie buried beneath five huge black crosses. There's a memorial chapel at the entrance. Another German cemetery lies close by at Saint-Germain-du-Pert.

Five miles from there, on the coast, is the **Rangers Museum** at Grandcamp Maisy. It commemorates this elite American unit and its attack on Pointe-du-Hoc on D-Day.

Musée des Rangers
30, quai Crampon
14450 Grandcamp-Maisy
Tel.: 02 31 92 33 51 - Fax: 02 31 22 64 34
e-mail: Grandcamp-Maisy @wanadoo.fr

Heading along the D514 you reach Vierville-sur-Mer and the **museum for the Omaha landings**. It's an impressive collection of equipment, uniforms, artillery, weapons and even aircraft engines.

Musée D-Day d'Omaha
Route de Grandcamp
14710 Vierville-sur-Mer
Tel./fax: 02 31 21 71 80

Open between March 30 and November 10.

Some three miles further down the D514 is Coleville-sur-Mer with its **American Cemetery**. It covers 20 hectares and there are more than 9,000 white crosses. Most of the soldiers buried here were killed during the landing. There's a **memorial chapel** to American youth.

Further inland, some twenty miles to the south west of Bayeux is a **memorial museum** dedicated to the fighting in bocage country.

Musée de la Percée du Bocage
14350 Saint-Martin-des-Besaces
Tel.: 02 31 67 52 78

The association Les **Amis du Suffolk Regiment** organize guided visits in the area of Colleville-Montgomery, especially the Hillmann fortified site, a German command post with numerous underground casemates. This place was taken by men of Suffolk Regiment on June 7, 1944.

IN THE LA MANCHE REGION

Passing into the La Manche region on the RN 13 you soon reach the Carentan canal and then Sainte-Marie-du-Mont with its **Utah Beach museum**. It is the only museum dedicated to the landings there in the entire region and the exhibits are first class. Allied assault equipment and German defensive equipment are presented and videos are shown in three languages. There's a panoramic view over Utah Beach itself and Pointe-du-Hoc.

Musée du Débarquement d'Utah-Beach
50480 Sainte-Marie-du-Mont
Tel.: 02 33 71 53 35 - 02 33 71 58 00

Opening hours: from March 15 to November 15, 10.00 to 12.30 and 14.00 to 17.30.

Another fascinating site is 10 miles to the northwest at Crisbecq. It's the **German battery of Azeville and Saint-Marcouf**. There were four casemates here, armed with 105 mm artillery and eight blockhouses with a garrison of 170 artillerymen. There is also a flak position, underground bunkers and stores.

Batterie d'Azeville et de Crisbecq
« Les Cruttes »
50310 Azeville
Tel.: 06 63 11 60 20 - 02 33 40 63 05
Fax: 02 33 40 63 06

Access to the underground sites is only possible with a guide. Visits last 45 minutes.